You Go Girl!

Compiled by Sonya Tinsley

Illustrated by Amy Dietrich

PETER PAUPER PRESS, INC.
WHITE PLAINS, NEW YORK

You GO Girl!

Introduction

Where have all the wallflowers
gone? One thing is certain,
you won't find any here. The
women in this volume remind
us with candor, wisdom, and
sometimes humor that we
alone are responsible for
making our lives into the works

of art we long for them to
become. Is it easy? Of course
not! But then neither is settling
for a life without passion and
self-fulfillment. Be inspired
by these women who have all
achieved their "impossible
dreams" and then "You Go, Girl!"

S. V. T.

Having company with yourself. My mamma can go in her room, sit on her balcony, and just watch the trees all day and not get bored. *That's* being grown.

Brandy

*W*hen I was 18 years old . . .
I took some time out and did not
date anybody for about a year and I
really focused on what I wanted to
do with my life and my career. I
found that that really helped me a
lot because that was how I found
myself. I realized that I didn't need
a man to make me happy or fulfill
the things that I wanted to fulfill.

Deborah Cox

And if you find your
soul mate, it's because you
have gotten to a place where
you've figured out what
your own soul is.

Sandra Bullock

J think everyone has a soulmate,
but I don't think you can
attract one until you say,
"I'm cool by myself."

Madonna

A guy might be able to slow
me down, but he's not
going to break me.

Toni Braxton

*y*ou can love someone
to the skies but it doesn't mean
you should be with him.
Love doesn't conquer all.

Mira Sorvino

*W*hen you meet another girl,
in two weeks you're not going
to call her your best friend.
So if you meet a guy, why . . .
would you give yourself—
something so precious—in
two or three weeks?

Chilli (of TLC)

I never thought that with the way I look, I would ever be in this position of being on a magazine cover, because I don't fit into the narrow definition of what is pretty. And then I thought, Why should I even try to think about that? Because I just am what I am, and I feel strong about myself, and some days I do feel beautiful and powerful . . .

Joan Osborne

J feel beautiful because of my heart. . . . I think it's the God in me that makes me beautiful. It doesn't really have anything to do with my physical features.

Lauryn Hill

*J*here's more to life
than cheekbones.

Kate Winslet

A happy heart comes first,
then the happy face.

Shania Twain

. . . *y*ou're only as good as
who you are at heart.

Tyra Banks

. . . *i*t was the happiness that
I thought could be attained from
achieving something, from the
praise and the fulfillment . . .
I didn't know that fame is the
same as not being famous—
only more so. Everything is
exactly the same, only amplified.

Alanis Morissette

*J*t seems like dealing with
success would be the easiest
part of music, but it's actually
the hardest part.

Monica

I went through a period
where I was being told nonsense.
They're gonna tell a young girl
her body's not beautiful?
You're talking about a life—
a human being!

Alicia Silverstone

*T*he most important thing is
to not lose sight of the work
and, it sounds corny, but be
yourself. They wanted me to
lighten my skin and to get a
nose job, but Hollywood
needs some real people.

Rosie Perez

J'm finally at a place where
if I meet someone who says,
"Whew! You are an *awfully* big
girl!" I'll just look them straight
in the eye and say, "I bet you
love that." . . . Not everyone
is supposed to be thin.

Emme Aronson (model)

I was raised by a strong working mom, so I always assumed that it was possible to be a woman and make your way in the world.

Natalie Merchant

Don't let anyone tell you that you have to be a certain way. Be unique. Be what you feel.

Melissa Etheridge

*Y*ou have one thing to fall
back on in this world, and
that's your intentions. That's
what matters most.

Drew Barrymore

J am ruled by the principle
of intention. Behind every cause
there is an intention. What you
put out comes back. Everything
that I do is done from the place
of intention that's going to mean
something for other people
as well as for myself.

Oprah Winfrey

*T*here's a lot happening in many of us. I think you have to celebrate every part. It's what you are. You have to try to find all those secret names.

Cassandra Wilson

*E*ach of us has that right, that possibility, to invent ourselves daily. If a person does not invent herself, she will be invented. Those who tower over us omnisciently and laugh will invent us. . . . So to be bodacious enough to invent ourselves is wise.

Maya Angelou

If you only try to please others,
you're going to resent those
people you're trying to please,
the ones who are often closest
to you. If you choose a path that
you yourself want to take, then
you're going to be much kinder
to the people in your life.

Sarah McLachlan

J think I encourage women to be who they want to be. I feel very tenacious and determined, and I'm someone for whom success has not happened overnight. I'm no great beauty; I'm no great intellect. I've got a bag of goods that are all right, and I've worked them, and that's good for young women to see.

Shirley Manson

I think focus is what has enabled me to excel in life. When I play basketball, there is absolutely nothing else on my mind but basketball. When I'm modeling, I'm focused entirely on modeling and doing the best I can . . . I also like to show girls that you can be tough and feminine too.

Lisa Leslie,
center for the WNBA's Los Angeles Sparks

J think I have much less talent
than I have guts. But because I
kept persevering, I took the little
bit of talent that I have and
made it the best it could be.

Sharon Stone

J'm a risk-taker.
My attitude is, go after what
you want. If you get it, fine,
if not, move on.

Vanessa Williams

I'm thrilled that women
are encouraged to follow their
dreams and I am equally pleased
that young men are getting
a new view of women: an
unapologetic woman.

Lucy Lawless

J think the New Lass has been around a long time. Some guys mistake it for either being too loud or being a bit tarty or a bit upfront, and they can be afraid of it because they're getting a taste of their own medicine.

Mel B (Scary Spice)

J only want to be like myself.
Why would I like to be Janet if
you've already got a Janet? Why
would anyone want to be a TLC?
You got the real one.

T-Boz (of TLC)

*I*t's important to be natural,
personality is like a muscle:
[People] have to use it and
work it for it to grow.

Geri (formerly Ginger Spice)

I don't waste much time—or very much time—wishing I was different. I am what I am, and I just make the best out of my personality.

Cher

J always thought I should
base how good I am on how
good I *feel* I am.

Neve Campbell

*Y*ou either shrink and hide
or you throw your shoulders
back and charge right in.
I learned that charging felt
more comfortable for me.

Minnie Driver

I allowed myself to be a diva
before I had any right to be.
The true divas have been divas all
their lives. They use this business
as an excuse to let it out.

Fiona Apple

𝕴 realized that a lot of
people think the grass is greener
on the other side . . . I used my
imagination . . . to make
the grass whatever color
I wanted it to be.

Whoopi Goldberg

Some people say I have attitude—maybe I do. But I think you have to. You have to believe in yourself when no one else does—that makes you a winner right there.

Venus Williams

*M*y huge turning point
was learning to trust myself
and feel as if I were good
enough. Not questioning
what I was doing, just going
ahead and doing it.

Peta Wilson

J knew how I wanted to live my life and what was important to me. It came from letting go of all that fear, of worrying about other people's perceptions, other people's anger. I realized that when I embraced who I was, who I really was, I became the best version of myself.

Gwyneth Paltrow

*F*ear doesn't even exist in my life
anymore. I respect people,
and respect and fear are two
different things. Fear is always
doing something wrong
because you're scared.
Respecting people, being good
to people, is courage.

Mary J. Blige

*L*ist the things you would
do if you weren't afraid.
Then do at least one of them.

Julia Sweeney,
comedian, actress, cancer survivor

How can I live my life in fear like that? The winners take risks. That's the only way to be.

Jennifer Lopez

*B*eing a queen doesn't mean that you never feel lonely or ugly or afraid. I'm afraid all the time. I'm afraid of being alone. I'm afraid of commitment. I'm afraid of becoming someone I'm not in the music business. I'm afraid of not having a child before I get too old. But none of these fears rules my life. Fear is a breeding ground for fear. If you don't control it, it will control you.

Queen Latifah

J had to face a lot of things
that I had avoided, and because
of that, I grew up. I realized that
everything was a choice: the
people I was with, what I was
doing with my life—everything.
The world was an open book.
Nothing was the same after that.

Shawn Colvin

J'm the type of person
who says, "Hey, this is the hand
I've been dealt; deal with it
Go on. Look ahead."

Faith Hill

*Y*ou know, my parents didn't do the greatest job, and a lot of parents don't, but I am aware of how my response to my past, as a child, has strengthened me into the person that I am today. And I don't regret anything that took place, or did not take place.

Gillian Anderson

*T*hings were tough, and you always say "God, I wish I did that differently." . . . But I'm kind of grateful for everything difficult that happened; it creates drive.

Jennifer Aniston

*Y*ou speak things into existence.
I know I do. I said I was going
to get a record deal, and grow
a seed, and continue to pursue
positive images and make
a change.

Erykah Badu

I take everything that I say very seriously. You can't take back words. And I don't do anything halfway.

Sarah Michelle Gellar

J knew I had to do something to survive . . . I also knew I was going to keep my integrity whatever I pursued. I wasn't going to sell myself short.

Dionne Farris

I just kept auditioning. I kept trying, and I kept believing in myself. I just kept knocking on doors that kept closing. . . . My coach said, "Vivica, your life could change in a day. If you're not ready, you won't be able to blame anybody but yourself."

Vivica A. Foxx

*D*on't let anybody take your dreams away from you. Talk about your goals. Let your friends and family know, even if they say, "Oh it's impossible." Nothing is impossible. Keep dreaming.

Celine Dion

*W*henever anybody is faced with a precarious or negative or odd situation in their life, they say, "If I had only done this or that." But everything for its purpose, I say, because you can't go back. Things just happen, and when good things happen you try to perpetuate that, and when bad things happen you try to learn from them and go on.

Julia Roberts

[Manners] say a lot about character—if you are kind or not, if you have enough sense to respect other people. . . . Whether you agree with who they are or what they're saying isn't the point; people should be respected just because.

Halle Berry

When I was eighteen, nineteen, twenty, I would see a woman baking cookies, or toting around a bunch of kids, or wearing lipstick and a tight dress, and I'd think, "Oh, please, baby—liberate yourself." I've come to realize, a few years later, who am I to decide what women's liberation looks or smells like?

Ani DiFranco

I've noticed a belief that
somehow optimism lacks
intelligence and that optimism
stems from a lack of experience
and naiveté. I don't believe that.
I believe optimism is a choice.
Cynicism isn't smarter,
it's just safer.

Jewel

*W*hat I say now is that the way
the world underestimates me
will be my greatest weapon.
People pat me on the head,
and I go to myself, oh, and aren't
they going to be surprised.

Calista Flockhart

Work is part of my genetic
code; work is in my blood.
My response to adversity
is always the same:
Work harder.

Janet Jackson

*I*t's not about being a star. I'd still be singing, dancing, writing songs, if this had never happened. . . . You take your talent and do your best and give it to people. I just want to make people, and myself, happy.

Mya

A lot of times when I meet people, they are surprised, like, "Oh, you know that?" I couldn't do this and not have some degree of intelligence.

Mariah Carey

I'm happy just knowing that
I have God in my life. . . .
It's about believing when you
ain't got nothing to believe in.

Whitney Houston

J was put on this earth
for something. I think
everyone is.

LeAnn Rimes

my life has been always about proving this thing: no one says you can do this . . . I've seen a lot of people do things that have never been done *all the time*. So if something hasn't been done, it means absolutely nothing to me.

Courtney Love

*B*oys had no interest in me. . . .
I went to five to seven agents
who weren't interested, and
now . . . All those boys who
didn't like me? This is the best
thing—to go and do great.

Jenna Elfman